The Simple Little Zucchini Book

35+ easy things to do with all that wonderful zucchini

Recipes, ideas, facts, and FUN!

Sorrel Mountain Press

To zucchini gardeners everywhere who understand the mixed delight and chagrin of finding yet more zucchini ready to harvest and use, faster than you may be ready for them!

CONTENTS

1) FUN ZUCCHINI FACTS

- ♥ Sprouts 4-9 days after planting
- ♥ Blooms in about 6 weeks
- ♥ 4-8 days from flower to fruit
- ♥ Fruit grows an inch or two per day
- ♥ Harvest ready 42-52 days from planting
- ♥ Each zucchini plant will yield up to 6-10 pounds of fruit in a season
- ♥ About 16 fruit per plant
- ♥ High in vitamins A&C, manganese, potassium, and fiber

2) MAIN DISHES and SIDES

You can add zucchini to many of your favorite recipes, from soups to stews to sloppy joes to whatever. Following are just a few ideas that you can adapt as you like.

We're not big on frying food, or sautéing. It makes too much grease, leaves the kitchen messier, and is a bigger bother, so wherever we mention boiling or steaming vegetables, if you prefer to sauté, that works too, just warm some oil, add the onion and garlic first, sauté a few minutes, add and brown any meat, and then add liquids and other vegetables or ingredients.

And, of course, substitute whatever vegetables and grains you have on hand or prefer, for the ones listed, but do keep the zucchini!

Enjoy and have fun!

Hearty Vegetable Soup

- 6 cups water or soup stock of your choice
- 2-3 large fresh tomatoes, chopped, or 1 15-ounce can chopped tomatoes
- 1 large onion, chopped
- 4 large carrots, sliced or chopped
- 2 cups chopped celery
- 1 butternut squash, halved, baked, and scooped out
- 2 cups zucchini, sliced in ¼ inch thick rounds, fresh or frozen
- 1 cup uncooked millet or quinoa
- 1 teaspoon each dried basil, thyme, and oregano
- 2 teaspoons cumin powder
- ¼ cup miso thinned with water
- salt and pepper to taste

Bring the water or stock to a boil in a large pot over high heat while adding the chopped tomatoes, onion, carrots, and celery. Turn heat to low and let simmer for 1½ to 2 hours. Meanwhile, halve the squash the long way, remove seeds, and place cut side down into baking pan filled with about ½ inch of water. Bake squash in oven at 350 degrees for about an hour, until soft. Remove from oven, let cool, then scoop out the flesh and reserve.

During last ½ hour or so of cooking soup, add the zucchini and millet or quinoa, allow to return to boil, reduce heat and simmer for 20-30 minutes more, until grain is cooked. Add seasonings and stir squash thoroughly into soup. Thin with water as desired. Keep warm until ready to serve. Just before serving, stir in miso.

Serve warm with bread, muffins, or crackers, and raw vegetables of your choice.

Sloppy Joes with Zucchini

- 1 pound ground beef, turkey, bison, or elk (or substitute 2-3 cups cooked grain)
- 2 cups sliced carrots
- 2 cups sliced celery
- 1 large onion, chopped
- 2 cloves garlic, minced
- 2-4 cups grated zucchini, fresh or frozen
- 1 6-ounce can tomato paste
- 1 tablespoon prepared mustard
- 2 tablespoons soy or Worcestershire sauce
- salt and pepper to taste

Brown meat in large 1 gallon cast iron skillet. Add all vegetables and 1-2 cups water. Bring to boil, reduce heat, and simmer for 45 minutes. Add tomato paste, mustard, and soy sauce. Simmer a few minutes longer. Remove from heat, salt and pepper to taste, and serve on burger buns.

Chili with Zucchini

- 1 pound ground beef, turkey, elk, bison, or 2-3 cups cooked grain
- 2-3 cups dry kidney beans, soaked in 8 cups water overnight, drained, rinsed, and cooked in fresh water to cover, 2-3 hours; or use equivalent in precooked canned beans
- 2 cups sliced carrots
- 1 medium to large onion, chopped
- 1-2 cloves garlic, minced
- 2 cups sliced celery
- 2-4 cups fresh or frozen grated or finely chopped zucchini
- 1 6-ounce can tomato paste
- 2 teaspoons cumin powder
- 1-2 teaspoons chili powder
- 1 teaspoon each dry basil and oregano
- salt and pepper to taste

Prepare kidney beans if using dry beans. Brown meat in large 1 gallon cast iron skillet. Add beans, all other vegetables, and enough water to cover. Bring to boil. Reduce heat. Simmer an hour or so. Add tomato paste and return to boil briefly. Remove from heat. Stir in seasonings. Salt and pepper to taste.

Zucchini Pizza

- Pizza crust
    - 1 teaspoon honey
    - 2 cups warm water
    - 1 ½ teaspoons active dry yeast
    - 2 teaspoons salt
    - 4 ½ cups whole wheat flour
    - 1 ½ tablespoons olive oil

- 1 6-ounce can tomato paste thinned with one can water, seasoned with 1 teaspoon each dry basil and oregano

- fresh or canned mushrooms, sliced
- black olives, sliced
- 2 cups fresh or frozen zucchini sliced into ⅛ - ¼ inch thick rounds

- 2 8-oz packages mozzarella cheese, grated

Dissolve honey and yeast in warm water. Mix salt and flour. Mix oil and honey-yeast mixture into flour-salt mixture. Knead 20 minutes. Let rise in warm location, 1½ hours, covered. Deflate by gently pushing down on dough. Let rise 45 minutes more. Cut into 2 pieces. Let rest until soft, about 10 minutes. Roll or press dough to fit 2 large oiled pizza pans. Cover with sauce, sliced zucchini, mushrooms, and olives. Sprinkle with cheese. Let rise 30 minutes. Preheat oven to 350 degrees and bake pizza about 20 minutes.

Or just add sliced zucchini to the top of any frozen pizza before baking, or to a pizza crust and toppings of your choice.

No Dough "Pizza"

- 2-3 medium zucchini, sliced in rounds ¼ inch thick
- other favorite pizza toppings
- 3-4 fresh medium tomatoes, sliced
- fresh basil leaves
- grated mozzarella cheese

Oil a 9 x 13 inch baking dish. Place zucchini slices to line the entire bottom of dish, overlapping as necessary to use all zucchini. Layer tomato slices on top of zucchini, and other toppings and basil leaves on top of tomatoes. Cover with lid or foil and bake for 30-45 minutes in oven preheated to 350 degrees. Remove cover. Sprinkle cheese over all. Heat another 10-15 minutes uncovered, until cheese is melted. Serve.

Simple Ratatouille

- 2-3 small to medium zucchini, chopped
- 1 eggplant, cubed
- 1 yellow summer squash, chopped
- 1 red pepper, sliced
- 2-3 chopped fresh tomatoes or 1 15-ounce can chopped tomatoes
- 1 large onion, chopped
- 1-2 teaspoons dry thyme
- grated cheese

Place all vegetables in an oiled casserole dish. Sprinkle with thyme. Cover and bake for 45 minutes in oven preheated to 350. Remove cover. Sprinkle all with grated cheese. Return to oven until cheese is melted. Serve.

Roasted Zucchini and other Vegetables

- 2 medium zucchini
- 4-6 medium size beets
- 1-2 medium potatoes
- 3-4 carrots
- 1-2 medium onions
- olive oil
- 1 tablespoon dry rosemary herb
- salt and pepper

Chop about 6-8 cups your choice of listed vegetables, or others, toss with ¼ - ½ cup olive oil, sprinkle with rosemary, salt, and pepper. Bake at 350 degrees in large covered casserole dish for 1 - 1½ hours. Remove cover, bake 20 minutes more. Serve.

Zucchini Frittata

- 1 cup chopped onions
- 2 cloves garlic, minced
- 2 cups sliced zucchini
- 1 teaspoon each dry basil, oregano, and thyme
- 12 eggs, beaten with 1 cup milk or water

Preheat oven to 350 degrees. In 9 x 13 inch glass baking dish, place all vegetables. Sprinkle with seasonings. Pour egg mixture over all. Mix lightly. Bake for 40-50 minutes or until set. Serve.

Zucchini and Parmesan with Spaghetti Noodles

- 2 medium zucchini, sliced into $\frac{1}{8}$ - $\frac{1}{4}$ inch thick rounds
- 2 tablespoons olive oil
- $\frac{1}{4}$ cup grated parmesan cheese, and more for topping
- 1 egg
- 1 pound spaghetti noodles
- salt

Steam zucchini in a small amount of water for 5-7 minutes. Drain and set aside. Mix together egg, 2 tablespoons olive oil, pinch salt, and ¼ cup grated parmesan cheese. Cook spaghetti following package directions. Drain and return to hot pan. Pour egg-cheese mixture onto hot noodles and briefly return pan to low heat, gently stirring for about 5 minutes until egg is cooked. Stir zucchini into pasta. Serve with more grated parmesan cheese sprinkled on top.

Zucchini in Spaghetti Sauce

- 2 6-ounce cans tomato paste
- 2 cups chopped fresh tomatoes, or 1 15-ounce can chopped tomatoes
- 1 onion, chopped
- 2 cloves garlic, minced
- 2 cups chopped mushrooms
- 1 cup chopped celery
- 1-2 small zucchini, sliced thin or grated, fresh or frozen
- 1 teaspoon each dry basil, oregano, and thyme
- salt and pepper to taste

Steam all vegetables in 1-2 cups boiling water until tender, about 10 minutes. Stir in tomato paste, tomatoes, and herbs. Thin to desired consistency. Bring gently to boil on medium heat. Reduce heat, and simmer about 10 minutes. Remove from heat. Salt and pepper to taste. Serve over pasta.

Sweet Vegetable Stew

- 2 onions, chopped
- 3 cloves garlic, minced
- 2 cups sliced carrots
- 1 cup chopped celery
- 1 stalk broccoli and/or 1-2 cups green beans, chopped
- 1 eggplant, diced
- 2-3 small zucchini, sliced thin
- 3 fresh large tomatoes, chopped, or 1 15-ounce can chopped tomatoes
- ¼ pound fresh mushrooms, sliced
- 1 6-ounce can tomato paste
- ¼ cup molasses, or a bit more to taste
- 1 tablespoon dry dill weed or 2 teaspoons dry oregano
- ½ cup water to thin if needed
- salt and pepper to taste

Steam together in 1-2 cups boiling water in 4 quart pot for 10-15 minutes: onions, garlic, carrots, celery, broccoli and/or green beans. Add eggplant, zucchini, tomatoes, and mushrooms. Steam for 15-20 minutes more until all vegetables are tender, adding more water if necessary. Stir in tomato paste, molasses, and dill weed or oregano. Heat to slow simmer on low to medium heat, adding water to desired thickness. Simmer 5-10 minutes. Remove from heat. Salt and pepper to taste.

Zucchini Almond Rice

- 1 cup almonds, toasted in pan in 300 degree oven for 10 minutes
- 2 cups uncooked brown rice
- 1 onion, chopped
- 1-3 cups zucchini, sliced thin, fresh or frozen
- 1-2 carrots, grated
- ¼ cup chopped fresh parsley

Sweet and Sour Sauce:

Mix together:
- ½ cup soy sauce
- ¼ cup cider vinegar
- ¼ cup honey
- ½ teaspoon ground ginger root

Bring rice, onion, zucchini, and 3 cups water to a boil. Turn heat to low and simmer for 35 minutes. When rice is done and all liquid absorbed, stir in almonds, carrots, and parsley. Turn heat off and let rice sit for 10 minutes, covered. Salt if desired. Serve with sweet and sour sauce.

Easy Oven Casserole

- 1 cup carrots, sliced ¼ inch thick
- 1 cup potatoes, sliced ⅛ - ¼ inch thick
- 1 cup sliced celery
- 1-2 small zucchini, sliced thin
- ¾ cup uncooked brown rice
- 1 cup sliced onion
- 3 cups canned chopped tomatoes and juice
- wheat germ or bread crumbs, if desired

Preheat oven to 350 degrees. Place layers as listed into an oiled 2 quart casserole dish. Cover. Bake 2 hours or until vegetables are tender and rice is done, adding more liquid if necessary. Uncover last 10 minutes.

Spanish Rice with Zucchini

- 3 cups uncooked brown rice
- 1 15-ounce can chopped tomatoes
- 3 cups chopped zucchini
- 1 onion, chopped
- 4 cups fresh mushrooms, chopped
- 4 stalks celery, chopped
- ½ cup fresh parsley
- 4 cups water
- 2 teaspoons oregano
- 2 teaspoons basil
- 2 teaspoons thyme
- 1 teaspoon chili powder
- salt and pepper to taste

Bring rice, tomatoes, all other vegetables, and 4 cups water to a boil in large pot. Reduce heat and simmer 35-40 minutes until rice is done, vegetables are tender, and liquid is absorbed. Remove from heat and add seasonings. Serve.

Quick Zucchini Pickles

- 3-4 cups zucchini sliced into ¼ inch thick rounds, or amount to almost fill a 1 quart canning jar
- 1 small onion, sliced thinly
- 3 cups white vinegar
- 1 cup dried cane juice or sugar
- 1 teaspoon salt

Pack zucchini and onion into a 1 quart heat-proof canning jar. In saucepan, heat vinegar, dried cane juice or sugar, and salt over medium heat until sugar is dissolved, about 5-10 minutes. Remove from heat and pour over zucchini/onions in jar, to cover them completely. Let cool uncovered. When cool, screw on lid and place in refrigerator. Can be eaten the next day. Will keep in refrigerator for about a month.

3) OTHER EASY MAIN DISH and SIDE IDEAS

❖ Add 1 cup grated zucchini to your favorite **meatloaf or meatball** recipe.

❖ Add 1 cup grated zucchini to your favorite **grain or meat burger** recipe.

❖ Add 1 cup grated zucchini to your favorite **potato pancake** recipe.

❖ Add grated zucchini to cooking chopped potatoes; mash together and add whatever you like for **mashed potatoes.**

❖ Or add chopped onion to cooking chopped potatoes and zucchini as above, mash, thin with milk or water, season as desired, and serve as **potato-zucchini soup.**

❖ Cut **zucchini lengthwise into spears**, brush with olive oil, grill or broil for a few minutes until tender. Season as desired.

OTHER EASY MAIN DISH and SIDE IDEAS (continued)

❖ Steam some grated zucchini with grated cabbage, chopped celery, onion, and mushrooms. Drain and mix a little bean paste and soy sauce into vegetables. Roll ¼ cup of mixture into each **eggroll** wrapper. Brush with oil and bake at 350 degrees for 20 minutes on each side.

❖ Add a layer of zucchini sliced in ¼ inch thick rounds between other layers in your favorite **lasagna** recipe.

❖ Add grated zucchini while cooking **scrambled eggs**.

❖ Add zucchini to **any soup, one pot rice, potato, or meat dish,** whether stovetop, oven, or crock pot, or add to any of your other favorite recipes.

4) QUICK BREADS, MUFFINS, COOKIES and PANCAKES

Try adding 1-2 cups grated zucchini to any cookie batter, quick bread or muffin recipe, or cake mix. Many quick bread, muffin, and cookie recipes can be adapted to adding grated zucchini. Here are a few ideas. If you like your breads, muffins, and cookies sweeter, increase the amount of sweetener a bit in these recipes.

Basic Zucchini Bread or Muffins

- 2 eggs
- ½ cup oil (optional) or other liquid if omitted
- ½ cup dried cane juice, or sugar
- 1 ½ cups whole wheat flour
- ½ teaspoon baking soda
- ½ teaspoon baking powder
- 1 teaspoon cinnamon
- ¼ teaspoon salt
- 1 cup fresh or frozen grated zucchini (thawed and drained)
- ½ cup each raisins and/or chopped nuts if desired
- for blueberry muffins, omit raisins and nuts and add 1 cup fresh or frozen blueberries to batter instead

Butter and flour a bread pan or muffin tins. Preheat oven to 325-350 degrees. Mix wet ingredients and dry ingredients separately, then mix all together. Stir in zucchini, raisins, and nuts, or berries. Spread batter in pan or muffin tins. Bake for 20-25 minutes for muffins or 35-40 minutes for bread, until pick comes out clean. Remove from oven. Remove from pan. Cool on rack.

Zucchini Cranana Nut Bread

- 2 eggs
- 1-2 bananas, mashed
- ¼ cup milk or water if needed
- ½ cup dried cane juice, or sugar
- 2 cups whole wheat flour
- ½ teaspoon baking powder
- ½ teaspoon baking soda
- ¼ teaspoon salt
- 1 cup fresh or frozen grated zucchini (thawed and drained)
- 1 cup fresh or frozen cranberries
- ½ cup chopped nuts

Butter and flour a bread pan. Preheat oven to 325-350 degrees. Mix wet ingredients and dry ingredients separately, then mix all together. Add a bit of milk or water or juice from thawed zucchini, if needed. Stir in zucchini, cranberries, and nuts. Spread batter in prepared pan. Bake for 30-35 minutes or until a pick comes out clean. Remove from oven. Remove from pan. Cool on rack.

Oatmeal Zucchini Cookies

- 1 cup butter, softened
- 1 cup dried cane juice, or brown sugar
- 2 eggs
- 1 teaspoon vanilla
- 2 cups whole wheat flour
- 1 teaspoon baking soda
- 1 teaspoon salt
- 1 ½ teaspoons cinnamon
- 3 cups rolled oats
- 1 cup grated zucchini
- 2 cups raisins
- 1 cup chopped walnuts

Preheat oven to 350 degrees and grease 2 cookie sheets. Cream butter, sugar, eggs, and vanilla. Stir in the rest of the dough ingredients. Stir in zucchini. Add raisins and nuts. Roll into walnut-sized balls and place about 2 inches apart on cookie sheets. Flatten slightly with fork. Bake 10-15 minutes, until lightly browned, switching pan positions halfway through baking time. Cool on sheets 5 minutes. Remove to racks. Cool.

Pancakes with Zucchini

- 4 eggs
- 2-2 ¾ cups water or milk
- 1 cup mashed banana or ½ cup dried cane juice or sugar
- 4 cups whole wheat flour
- 4 tablespoons baking powder
- ½ teaspoon salt
- 2 cups grated zucchini
- fresh or frozen fruit, if desired

Start heating griddle or frying pan on medium heat. Mix eggs with milk or water and sugar or banana. Mix dry ingredients. Add wet ingredients to dry ingredients and mix well. Stir in grated zucchini and fruit. Add more liquid to thin or a bit more flour to thicken, as needed. Pour about ¼ cup of batter for each pancake onto a hot buttered griddle or pan. Fry on each side until browned and cooked through. Serve with maple syrup.

5) OTHER SIMPLE USES FOR ZUCCHINI

❖ Feed very large overgrown zucchini to your or your neighbors' chickens.

❖ Donate zucchini to your local food pantry or soup kitchen.

❖ Give them to neighbors, friends, family, strangers, coworkers, church or club members.

❖ Trade for other garden produce.

❖ Hand out to parents on Halloween.

❖ Freeze 2-4 cups raw grated zucchini in freezer bags to use over the winter in the recipes in this book.

❖ Freeze zucchini sliced into ¼ inch thick rounds. Blanch for 3 minutes in boiling water, cool quickly in cold water, drain, and freeze in flat layers in 1 gallon freezer bags in a stack in the freezer to use in recipes in this book or your own favorites!

Enjoy and have fun with your zucchini riches!

☺

www.ingramcontent.com/pod-product-compliance
Lightning Source LLC
Chambersburg PA
CBHW030305030426
42337CB00012B/591